I'll
Catch
the
Moon

By Nina Crews

Greenwillow Books, New York

Special thanks to Devika Jutagir, who modeled for the
book; her mother, Hattie Jutagir; and her cousin,
Diana Phillips. Also thanks to Alexandra McGovern
and Donald Crews for their assistance.

The art was prepared as collages made from color and black-and-white
photographs. Photographs of the earth, the astronaut, and the close-
up of the moon's surface are courtesy of NASA. All other photographs
are by the author. The text type is ITC Cheltenham Bold.

Library of Congress Cataloging-in-Publication Data

Crews, Nina.
I'll catch the moon / Nina Crews.
p.   cm.
Summary: A child imagines going into outer space, catching
the moon, and taking it on an around-the-world adventure.
ISBN 0-688-14134-X (trade).   ISBN 0-688-14135-8 (lib. bdg.)
[1. Moon—Fiction.   2. Imagination—Fiction.]   I. Title.
PZ7.C8683If   1996   [E]—dc20   95-12346   CIP   AC

For Amy

Outside my window
I see the city and the sky.

Honk, blink, stop, go.
City moves below me.

Tall buildings climb into the air.
The moon floats
above.

Moon.
Silver shining like a quarter.
I would like to put it
in my pocket.

I've seen pictures of the moon.
Men on the moon.
The man in the moon.
And a cow jumping
over it.

Sometimes it looks very big
and sometimes
very small.

I'd like to catch that moon.
I'll build a ladder into
outer space.

I'll go past buildings, past helicopters, airplanes, and clouds.

I'll climb, climb, and climb.
The stars will watch me,
and a comet will guide
my way.

The moon and I will travel together. Round and round the world we'll go.

We'll run, jump, skip, hop
from night to day
and day to night.

We'll play hide-and-seek
in the clouds.

Then I'll go back home.
My family will be
missing me.

From my
window
I'll wave to
the moon
passing above
me at night.

That's how it will be.
I think I'll go soon.
And then I'll catch the moon.